SNOW and ICE

Canadian Winter Weather

Nicole Mortillaro

Scholastic Canada Ltd.

Toronto New York London Auckland Sydney
Mexico City New Delhi Hong Kong Buenos Aires

For Dad
Che fantastica storia è la vita.

Photo Credits

Cover image: Dex Image/Fotosearch; page iv: Firstlight; page 2: Firstlight; page 3: Dex Image/Fotosearch; page 10: Courtesy Parks Canada; page 12: Firstlight; page 13: Detail, courtesy of Environment Canada; page 14: Phill Snel/Canadian Press; page 19: Courtesy Electron Microscopy Unit, ARS, USDA; page 20: Jacques Boissinot/Canadian Press; page 21: Detail, courtesy of NB Power; page 23: Bill Sykes/Associated Press; page 25: Courtesy of Hydro Quebec; page 28: Firstlight; page 29: Detail, courtesy of Jerry Shields; page 31: Courtesy of Vincent Chan; page 33: Chuck Stoody/Canadian Press; page 34: Courtesy of Jamie Pye; Page 38: Provided by the SeaWiFS Project, NASA/Goddard Space Flight Center, and ORBIMAGE; page 40: Courtesy of Chris Gray ©; pages 41 and 43: Courtesy Peter Jeffery; page 44: Courtesy of Stephen Mayne; page 45: Courtesy of George Kourounis; page 46: Courtesy Alister Ling; page 47: Courtesy Dan Kelly, National Weather Service; page 49: Courtesy George Kourounis; page 50: Courtesy of NOAA's National Climatic Data Center; page 51: Detail, Nicole Mortillaro; page 52: Courtesy James Colwell; page 55: Courtesy Herb Thoms, Environment Canada; page 56: Courtesy of the Niagara Falls Public Library; page 58: Clair Israelson, Canadian Avalanche Association.

Special thanks to Geoff Coulson, Ian Hickey and Bob Robichaud for all of their expertise and assistance.

Library and Archives Canada Cataloguing in Publication

Mortillaro, Nicole, 1972-
Snow and ice: Canadian winter weather / Nicole Mortillaro.
(Canada close up)
ISBN 0-439-95746-X
1. Winter—Canada—Juvenile literature. 2. Canada—Climate—Juvenile literature. I. Title. II. Series: Canada close up (Markham, Ont.)
QC981.3.M675 2005   j551.6971   C2005-901033-9

Text copyright © 2005 by Nicole Mortillaro.
All rights reserved.

No part of this publication may be reproduced or stored in a retrieval system, or transmitted in any form or by any means, electronic, mechanical, recording, or otherwise, without written permission of the publisher, Scholastic Canada Ltd., 175 Hillmount Road, Markham, Ontario L6C 1Z7, Canada. In the case of photocopying or other reprographic copying,a licence must be obtained from Access Copyright (Canadian Copyright Licensing Agency), 1 Yonge Street, Suite 1900, Toronto, Ontario M5E 1E5 (1-800-893-5777).

6 5 4 3 2   Printed in Canada   05 06 07 08 09

Table of Contents

Introduction

What does wintertime in Canada mean to you? Does it mean skating and building snow forts? Or does it mean bundling up to stay warm? Maybe it means both!

Sometimes we might feel like it's too cold to play outside. And sometimes snow and ice can make travelling dangerous.

But wintertime in Canada can also be a lot of fun. We can play in the snow, ski, snowboard, snowmobile or race a toboggan down a hill. We can catch snowflakes on our tongues and see frost-covered trees sparkle in the sun.

Come explore our winter wonderland!

Chapter 1

Canada's Climate

Canada is known for its chilly **climate**. Climate is what we call the weather in an area over a long time. Many people think Canada's climate is always cold and snowy, but we get many warm and sunny days, too.

Canada has four seasons: spring, summer, fall and winter.

In the spring, temperatures start to rise. Flowers and trees begin to bloom. In the summer, it gets even warmer, and some places in Canada get quite hot. In the fall, most trees lose their leaves, and temperatures begin to drop. Winter in Canada usually means much colder weather and lots of snow.

Our seasons change depending on which way Earth is tilted as it orbits the Sun. When Canada is tilted toward the Sun, the Sun's rays hit us straight on and we get warm weather. When we are tilted away from the Sun, we get the Sun's rays at an angle.

That's when it's time to bundle up!

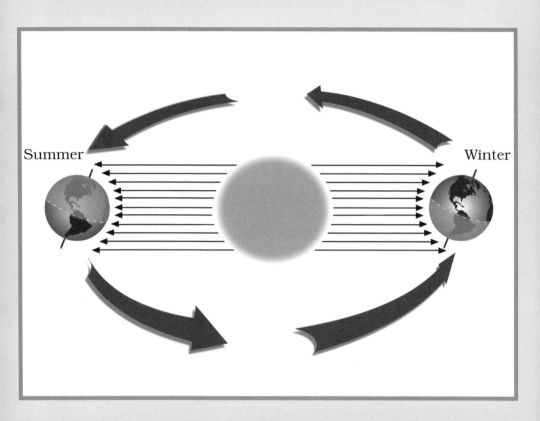

Summer

Winter

● It's not Earth's distance from the Sun that gives us winter. In fact, in winter we are closest to the Sun. We get cold weather because we are tilted away from the Sun and get less of its warmth.

The Sun warms Earth's surface, and the heat from the land and water warms the air above. As air heats up, it becomes lighter and rises. As it cools, it grows heavier, and starts to fall.

Air usually flows from areas of higher weight or pressure to areas of lower weight or pressure. This creates the wind that we feel when we go outside. When differences between areas of high and low air pressure are greater, they make very strong winds.

Earth's weather is moved around by **jet streams**. Jet streams are fast winds that blow from west to east. They are high in our **atmosphere**, and they're always moving. Because they move, they carry different weather systems with them. Earth has four jet streams, including a powerful one that flows above Canada.

Because Canada is so big, the weather is very different from one part of our country to the next.

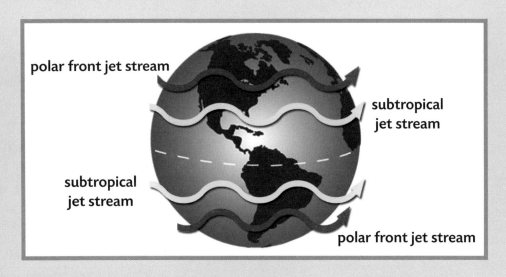

polar front jet stream

subtropical
jet stream

subtropical
jet stream

polar front jet stream

● Earth has four jet streams. The polar front jet stream that blows above Canada has wind speeds that begin at 110 km per hour, but can reach more than 300 km per hour.

Our country touches the Pacific, Atlantic and Arctic Oceans. The Pacific Ocean on the west coast is warm. The Atlantic Ocean on the east coast is cold, but it has a warm stream of water (the Gulf Stream) running through it. The Arctic Ocean, on our north coast, is very cold.

The temperature of the water in each ocean affects the temperature of the air above it.

An **air mass** is a large area of air that has the same amount of moisture and the same temperature all the way through. Air masses form over large bodies of water or areas of land that are mostly all one temperature.

The jet stream that flows above Canada carries these air masses away from the oceans and lands where they formed and moves them around our country.

In the winter, Canada's Arctic is tilted the farthest away from the Sun. Because it gets less direct sunlight than southern Canada, it is usually colder.

The air masses that form above the frozen Arctic land and the cold Arctic Ocean bring Canada its chilliest winter weather.

Weather fact:

In the winter, you might hear people talk about **wind chill.** Meteorologists use it to tell us what temperature it feels like with the wind blowing. The thermometer may say it's -10°C outside, but with a strong, cold wind blowing, it could feel like it's -25°C.

Usually the coldest air masses stay in the north, and the warmest ones stay in the south, but sometimes the jet streams bring us surprises.

A perfect example of this happened in January 2005. On January 13, Toronto saw an all-time high temperature of 17.5°C. It felt like spring! Meanwhile, on the exact same day, it was a chilly -41.8°C in Whitehorse, Yukon. Two weeks later Toronto was colder than Whitehorse! In Toronto it was -15°C. Whitehorse was -4°C!

● Above is a picture of a chinook arch. These types of clouds happen on the east side of the Rocky Mountains. They are a sign that warm chinook winds have come to southern Alberta. When a chinook happens in the winter, it can raise the temperature by more than 20°C in a few hours. On January 11, 1983, a chinook made the temperature in Calgary rise from -17°C to 13°C in just 4 hours — that's a difference of 30°C!

It's important to protect yourself on really cold days. Here are some ways to stay safe in cold weather.

✳ Have a snack before going out. This will give you lots of energy to keep your body warm.

✳ Wear a few layers of clothing. The air that is trapped between the different layers of clothing can help to keep you warmer.

✳ Make sure you always wear a hat and mitts. Even though you might not like wearing a hat, it keeps in a lot of your body heat.

✳ If you feel too cold, or if your hands or feet start to feel numb, go inside.

Chapter 2

Snow and Rain

If you have lived in Canada in the winter, you know what snow is. But where does it come from?

Snow is a type of **precipitation**. Precipitation is water that falls from the clouds. It can fall as rain, snow or even hail. In winter we can get all kinds of precipitation.

● In 1999 Toronto called in the army to help it dig out from the city's worst snowstorm ever! In the first two weeks of January more than 70 cm of snow fell. Toronto usually only gets 38 cm in the whole month! Subways were shut down and schools were closed. Many people couldn't get to work. It took the city almost two weeks to recover.

Heat from the Sun causes the water in our streams, lakes and rivers to change into a gas called **water vapour.** When water vapour rises into our atmosphere, it cools. As the vapour cools, it turns into water droplets or ice crystals, depending on the temperature. These droplets and crystals collect together with things like dust particles to make the clouds we see.

But how is snow made? Most precipitation starts off as ice crystals high up in the clouds where it is very cold. The ice crystals grow as they pick up water vapour. The crystals begin to stick together. When they get heavy enough, they fall to the ground. If the temperature near the ground is cold, the crystals stay cold and we get snow. If it is warm, we get rain.

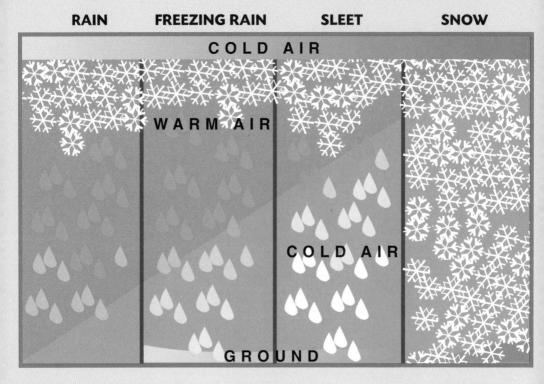

| RAIN | FREEZING RAIN | SLEET | SNOW |

COLD AIR

WARM AIR

COLD AIR

GROUND

Precipitation often begins as ice crystals. If the crystals fall through warm air, they melt and we get rain. If the air is warm, but the ground is cold, the rain will refreeze and turn to ice — that's freezing rain. If the crystals melt as they fall through a layer of warm air, but partly refreeze when they hit a layer of cold air, we get sleet. If the crystals only fall through cold air, and don't melt, we get snow.

Water freezes at 0°C. If rain falls through air that is colder than that temperature, it starts to freeze. If snowflakes fall through air that is warmer than that temperature, they start to melt.

So as precipitation falls it may change from ice to water, or water to ice — sometimes more than once.

Sleet is a mixture of rain and snow. It happens when rain falls through cold air and partly freezes, or when snow falls through warm air and partly melts. It feels slushy, and it can make your hat and mittens very cold and soggy.

Freezing rain starts off as ice crystals. The crystals melt when they fall through a warm layer of air and become rain. But then, just before the rain reaches the ground, it meets a freezing layer of air. The rain refreezes as it touches something cold, like a car or the pavement. It can make the ground very slippery and dangerous to walk on.

Weather fact:

Canada's biggest recorded snowflake fell in Halifax, Nova Scotia, on February 22, 1986. It was 5 cm across — that's bigger than two loonies side by side!

Winter in Canada may also bring us snow pellets. They look like little snowballs. Snow pellets can happen when strong winds inside a cloud bounce the ice crystals around. Water droplets freeze around the crystals, which grow in size before falling to the ground.

Snow pellets can also happen when snowflakes melt and then refreeze before hitting the ground.

● Wilson "Snowflake" Bentley spent 47 years studying snowflakes. He took over 5,000 photographs of them. What did he discover? That no two snowflakes are alike!

Chapter 3

Ice Storms

Ice storms bring some of our worst winter weather. They make roads slippery and dangerous. The weight of the ice on power lines can break them. If this happens, there may be no heat or power for our homes.

You are most likely to see an ice storm if you live in southeastern Canada. They usually happen between Ontario and Newfoundland.

Eastern Quebec has many ice storms. This is because it lies in a valley. The air in the valley is colder than the air above and around it. So as rain falls, it freezes when it hits this cold area.

Atlantic Canada, especially Newfoundland, gets more freezing rain than any other area in Canada. This is because Newfoundland has milder winters, with temperatures from 0°C to -7°C. The moist and fairly mild air from the Atlantic Ocean often brings rain, but when it reaches Newfoundland, the cooler land temperature freezes the precipitation as it hits the ground.

Ice storms can cause a lot of damage. The weight of ice on the trees often causes branches to break off. The branches can crush houses and cars.

Ice storms can be very hard to predict. This is because they happen when the temperature is close to 0°C. That is the freezing point of water.

If the temperature on the ground is above 0°C, ice crystals will melt and turn into water. If it is below 0°C on the ground, water droplets will freeze and turn to ice. This means that a 1° difference in temperature can give us snow, freezing rain, sleet or rain.

Weather fact:

In Canada, winter weather is blamed for the deaths of about 100 people every year. That's more than from hurricanes, tornadoes, floods and lightning combined!

The photo above shows hydro towers in Quebec during the 1998 ice storm. The weight of the ice made them collapse. This caused power outages across the province.

One of Canada's worst ice storms happened in 1998. For five days in January, freezing rain, ice pellets and snow fell in eastern Ontario and Quebec. The weight of the ice crumpled hydro towers and pulled down power lines.

The storm hit an area in Canada and the United States where many people live. More than four million people lost their power. Some people didn't have their power back for weeks!

Farmers also suffered. Many had to share power generators to run milking machines and to provide heat for newborn piglets. Quebec makes more than 70% of the world's maple syrup. But this storm destroyed many maple trees.

The ice storm of 1998 affected more people than any other weather event in Canadian history.

In April 1956, St. John's, Newfoundland, was hit by an ice storm that lasted more than 43 hours. More than 200 000 people were left without power.

How bad was the ice storm of 1998?

❄ 25 people died

❄ about 900 000 homes in Quebec and 100 000 homes in Ontario had no power

❄ about 100 000 people had to live in emergency shelters

❄ millions of trees were destroyed

❄ 120 000 km of power lines and telephone cables were destroyed

In 2002, another terrible storm hit the same area. An ice storm swept through Gander and ice covered the buildings, hydro wires and trees.

Chapter 4

Blizzards

Snowy days can be a lot of fun. We can toboggan, throw snowballs and build snowmen.

But sometimes we get blizzards, and they can be dangerous. Blizzards mean strong winds and snow. They can make it unsafe to travel.

Blizzards are more than just snow storms. They must also have the following ingredients:

✳ snow or blowing snow

✳ strong winds

✳ less than 1 km of visibility (you can't see a kilometre ahead of you)

✳ a wind chill of -25°C or colder

✳ all the above, for four hours or more

Each winter, Canada has many blizzards. They usually happen in the southern prairies, Atlantic Canada and the eastern Arctic. Blizzards are rare in British Columbia, the western Northwest Territories and the Yukon.

Blizzards in the Prairies and eastern Arctic are common because they often get very cold and windy Arctic air. This air can quickly turn a regular snowfall into a blizzard. In Atlantic Canada, blizzards happen when very cold and windy Arctic air meets with warm, moist air that has moved up from the south.

In May 2001, Resolute Bay, Nunavut had a blizzard that lasted 3 days!

In 1947, a horrible blizzard hit the Prairies. It lasted 10 days. Roads into Regina, Saskatchewan were blocked. Just outside of Moose Jaw, Saskatchewan, a farmer had to cut a hole in his barn roof so he could get in to milk his cows!

Weather fact:

Have you ever noticed that it seems quieter after snow has fallen? That's because the snow hasn't settled yet. The snow absorbs sounds. It actually is quieter.

Blizzards in British Columbia may be rare, but they still happen. In 1996, Victoria and Vancouver received more than 80 cm of snow between Christmas and New Year's. This beat their old record of 53 cm.

● The blizzard that hit British Columbia in 1996 shut down roads and stranded many travellers.

Victoria was at a standstill. Even ambulances and police cars couldn't move. Many people didn't even have shovels. Ice pellets made the snow very heavy. Roofs collapsed. The whole thing cost the city millions of dollars. It was British Columbia's worst snowfall in 80 years.

● From February to April 2004, huge snowdrifts closed parts of the Trans Labrador Highway. In April, heavy machinery was finally used to reopen the road.

It seems like the Atlantic Provinces get the worst weather. Not only do they get hurricanes in the summer, but they also get strong blizzards in the winter.

In December 2004, a blizzard hit the east coast of Canada. Charlottetown, PEI, got more than 54 cm of snow, and Moncton, New Brunswick, got 48 cm.

Then, in January 2005, three more blizzards struck Atlantic Canada in just three weeks! In some places winds whipped up to 100 km an hour. That's as fast as a car driving down the highway! Charlottetown and Moncton got over 90 cm more snow. Imagine trying to shovel that!

Weather fact:

Why is it that sometimes we can make snowballs and other times we can't? It's because snowflakes are stickier when there is a lot of moisture. If the atmosphere is cold and dry, the snow isn't "wet" enough to stick together. We call dry snow "powder" snow.

Some other big blizzards:

✳ St. John's, Newfoundland, February 16, 1959: Six people died, 70,000 people lost power.

✳ Iqaluit, Nunavut, February 8, 1979: People were forced to stay inside for 10 days as temperatures fell to -40°C. Winds of 100 km/h hour swept snow around the community.

✳ Winnipeg, Manitoba, November 7 and 8, 1986: About 30 cm of snow fell on the city over a 24-hour period.

Sometimes a snowstorm might not have all of the ingredients necessary for a blizzard, but it can still be dangerous. Some severe snowstorms are caused by lake effect snow.

Lake effect snow forms near large lakes. In the winter, the lakes can warm the cooler air right above them. This air rises, and as it meets cooler air, it begins to form clouds.

Water vapour builds up in the clouds. The clouds are then pushed by the wind. Snow starts to fall. This is common around the Great Lakes region in Ontario.

Weather fact:

Is it ever too cold to snow? Not really. It might seem that it doesn't snow on very cold days. That's because only a small amount of water vapour can exist in very cold air. So snowfall on cold days is not very common.
But in Eureka, Nunavut, 15.2 cm of snow fell on December 23, 1983 when it was a chilly -21°C.

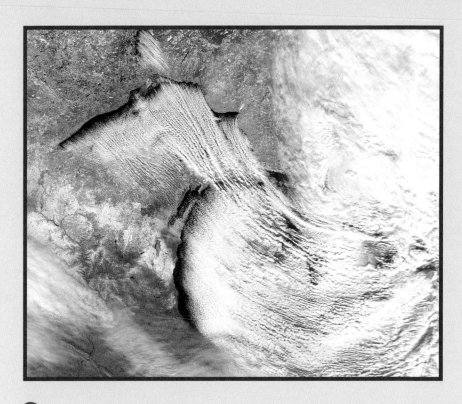

This is a picture taken from a satellite. It shows a snow squall that is happening over the Great Lakes.

Snow squalls also happen around the Great Lakes. They are a stronger type of lake effect snow. A squall has very high winds and heavy snow. The winds cause the snow to blow around very fast, and this makes it difficult for people to see where they are going. Because of this, squalls can be as dangerous as blizzards.

Sometimes we get snowstorms called Alberta Clippers. They start east of the Rockies, then head southeast, across southern Canada and the northern United States.

These storms move fairly fast and don't drop much snow. However, they do bring cold air from the Arctic and sometimes high winds. These winds blow around the snow that does fall. This can create blizzard-like weather.

How to keep safe in a blizzard:

❋ Stay indoors.

❋ Make sure your pets are inside.

❋ Keep extra batteries for flashlights in case the power goes out.

❋ Be careful when you shovel. You can get hurt if you pick up too much snow.

Chapter 5

Winter Wonders

Lots of strange things happen in the winter — it's not all about blizzards and ice storms. Some types of weather can be scary or destructive, while others can be beautiful and rare. Sometimes they can be both.

Because we have more hours of darkness in the winter, it is a good time to catch a glimpse of auroras. The auroras that we see in Canada are called Aurora Borealis, or the northern lights.

Auroras are usually caused by a big explosion on the Sun's surface. If Earth is in the right place when this happens, the particles from the explosion get caught in our atmosphere at the north and south poles. We see these particles as beautiful lights in the night sky. What is interesting is that the lights seem to move.

The northern lights are usually seen in northern Canada in places like the Yukon, Northwest Territories, Nunavut and northern Quebec.

Aurora Borealis light up a harbour in Yellowknife, Northwest Territories.

But in November 2004, a big explosion on the Sun sent lots of particles in our atmosphere. The auroras could be seen as far south as Florida in the United States!

Sundogs over a snowy field.

Ice crystals in our atmosphere can
also make a beautiful display. It is
more common to see these displays
in winter. This is because the Sun
is lower in the sky, and its light
comes through the atmosphere on
more of an angle. When the light
hits these crystals right, you might
see sundogs, halos or even sun
pillars.

Sundogs are sometimes called "mock suns." They are called this because they look like fake suns on either side of the real Sun.

Sun halos are rainbow-like halos that circle the Sun. Light is made up of different colours. If the Sun is in the right position, it separates these colours. Halos happen when high, thin clouds are in the sky. Sometimes you might even see a halo around the moon at night.

The Sun with a halo around it.

A sun pillar stretches high above the horizon.

Sun pillars can be seen at sunrise or sunset. As the Sun hovers near the horizon, a beautiful pillar of light stretches up into the sky.

A rare find during winter is a snow roller. It is a layer of snow that has been rolled up by the wind. A snow roller looks like a log that is hollow in the middle.

● There are several snow rollers in this farmer's field. It must have been a windy day!

What does it take for a snow roller to form?

❋ light, new snow

❋ temperatures rising to just 1 or 2 degrees above zero

❋ strong winds blowing across an open space.

The strong winds catch a layer of the snow and roll it up, just like a roll of sod.

If you are close to open water, steam fog is something else that you might see on a cold winter day. It happens when cold, dry air moves across water that is about 10°C warmer than the air.

The winds need to be calm for the "steam" to stay above the water. The warm, moist air rises, meets the cold air and cools. It looks like steam rising off the water.

Steam fog over Lake Ontario.

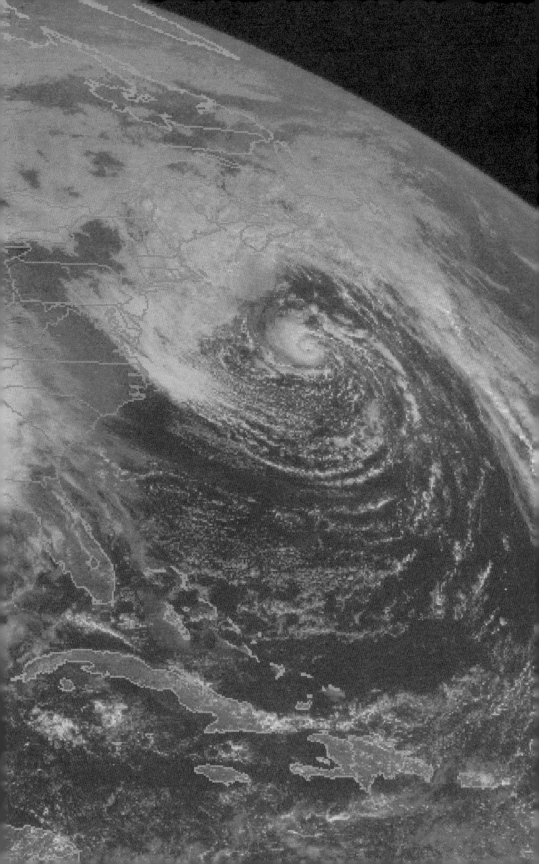

Chapter 6

Extreme Weather

Each winter Canada has many severe storms. Some may be called blizzards, but other storms are also known as nor'easters or weather bombs. And one winter there was a storm so bad that it was called the "perfect storm."

Nor'easters are a type of blizzard. They usually happen between October and April in the Atlantic Provinces. They bring heavy rain or snow. The storm gets its name from the winds that blow in from the northeast. These storms need warm air and moisture from the Atlantic.

When this air meets with cold Arctic air, watch out! You've got a chilly, windy nor'easter!

● The nor'easter that hit the Atlantic provinces in 1991 left the area buried in snow. In the picture above, in front of the middle house, you can just see the top of a snow-covered car.

In February 2004, a nor'easter hit Nova Scotia. In just one day Halifax got 88.5 cm of snow. It became the biggest city in the world to get so much snow in just one day!

In October 1991, a severe nor'easter swept through the north Atlantic. It had three powerful ingredients. One was cold Arctic air that was pushed down toward the east coast. The other was a storm off the coast of Nova Scotia. The third, and most important, was the storm that was left from Hurricane Grace.

Once the three parts joined, they created a storm that many people have called the "perfect storm." Ocean waves became very powerful and pounded the coast. Twelve people in Canada and the United States lost their lives in the storm.

A weather bomb is a storm that gets strong fast and brings very high winds and lots of moisture.

These types of storms need very specific conditions to happen, so they are rare. Weather bombs can bring heavy rain or snow.

A weather bomb hit Nova Scotia in February 2004. It brought several blizzards with it. The blizzards closed schools and buildings for almost a week!

Weather fact:

A wave more than 9 m high was recorded off the coast of Nova Scotia during the "perfect storm" of 1991. That's as tall as a three-storey building, and one of the tallest waves on record.

Ice jams are another winter worry. As thick ice breaks up and floats down a river, it can get stuck and block the flow of water. This can cause serious flooding, and is very dangerous for towns near water.

● An ice jam created a strange winter flood in Badger, Newfoundland, in February 2003. Ice jammed the three rivers near the town. The river water suddenly rose 2.5 m and broke through the ice. Then it began to flood the town. Over the next few days, temperatures dropped below -20°C. The flood water surrounding the town's houses and businesses froze. People couldn't go home for almost two weeks, and many of their houses were destroyed.

If you've ever been to Niagara Falls, you might have a hard time believing that the water could stop. But it has happened. In 1848, ice jammed the Niagara River. People woke up to hear . . . nothing. They even walked down to the bottom of the falls. A day later, the water pushed the ice through and water fell again.

● Until three people died in 1912, visitors to Niagara Falls were allowed to walk out across the huge ice bridges that would form when it was very cold.

Weather fact:

Even though it is rare, we can still get thunderstorms in winter. This is sometimes called "thundersnow."

Winter can also bring flash freezes. These happen when temperatures have been above 0°C, and the snow has begun to melt. The melting snow makes the streets and sidewalks wet.

Then, suddenly, the temperature falls to below freezing. Wet surfaces quickly freeze and become covered in ice. Flash freezes can cause lots of traffic accidents and make sidewalks very slippery.

● This is a controlled avalanche. It was started on purpose, probably by using explosives. This is often done when an area close to a road seems at risk for an avalanche. The road is closed until the avalanche is over.

If you're ever near a mountain and you hear a loud rumbling sound, watch out! An avalanche may be happening. Each year in Canada, about 13 people die in avalanches.

Avalanches happen when a lot of snow or ice slides down the side of a mountain. Sometimes we get them because new snow that is not very moist sits in a layer on top of older, drier snow.

This new snow may not really settle, so it could slide down the older snow. Avalanches may also start because of a loud noise, a heavy snowfall or warmer weather. In an avalanche the snow falls very fast and people can get trapped underneath it.

Canada's worst avalanche was the one at Rogers Pass, British Columbia in 1910. Sixty-two workers died when they were trying to remove snow from an earlier avalanche that had covered railway tracks.

Weather winners:

Sunniest winter: Calgary, AB
Windiest winter: St. John's, NL
Coldest winter: Yellowknife, NT
Mildest winter: Victoria, BC
Most snow days: Val D'Or, QC
Snowiest city: Gander, NL

Glossary

air mass: a large area of air that has the same amount of moisture and the same temperature all the way through

atmosphere: the mixture of gases that surround our planet

climate: the weather in an area over a long period of time

jet stream: fast moving winds, high above Earth, that flow from west to east

precipitation: water that falls, in a variety of forms, from clouds

water vapour: a gas that is formed when water is heated; water vapour forms clouds

wind chill: what temperature it feels like with the wind blowing